The GIRLS' Book 2

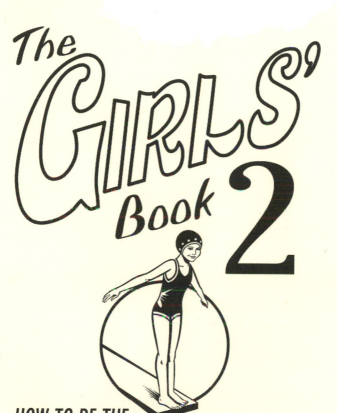

HOW TO BE THE
BEST AT EVERYTHING
AGAIN

Written by Sally Norton
Illustrated by Katy Jackson
Edited by Philippa Wingate
Designed by Zoe Quayle

The GIRLS'
Book 2

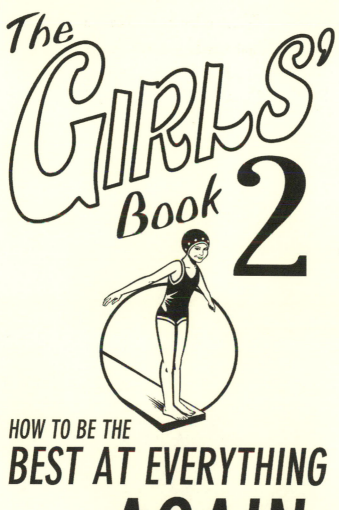

HOW TO BE THE
BEST AT EVERYTHING
AGAIN

Buster Books

For the delightful Kate Jeffrie

First published in Great Britain in 2008 by Buster Books,
an imprint of Michael O'Mara Books Limited,
9 Lion Yard, Tremadoc Road, London SW4 7NQ

 www.busterbooks.co.uk

 Buster Children's Books

 @BusterBooks

Text and illustrations copyright © Buster Books 2008
Cover designed by Angie Allison (from an original design by www.blacksheep-uk.com)
Cover illustration: Paul Moran

A CIP catalogue record for this book is available from the British Library.

ISBN: 978-1-78055-272-9

Printed and bound by CPI Group (UK) Ltd.,
108 Beddington Lane, Croydon, CR0 4YY, United Kingdom.

NOTE TO READERS

The publisher and author disclaim any liability for accidents or injuries that may occur as a result of the information given in this book.

To be the best at everything, you'll need to use your best common sense at all times, particularly when heat or sharp objects are involved, and follow safety precautions and advice from responsible adults at all times. Always wear appropriate safety gear, stay within the law and local rules, and be considerate of other people.

CONTENTS

HOW TO BE THE BEST CHEERLEADER

Experienced cheerleaders put on amazing shows that include cartwheels, handsprings and complicated jumps. If you can master the seven basic cheerleading moves described here, you can put them together in a pom-pom-tastic routine.

Practise to some loud, funky music with a great beat.

The High V. Stretch both arms up and out in a V-shape above your head. At the same time, jump your feet out to the sides. Hold for a count of three then shake your pom-poms. Then drop your arms to your sides.

The L-Motion. Jump your feet together. Raise your left arm straight above your head and your right arm out to the side, so your arms form an L-shape. Hold for three, then shake your pom-poms. Then reverse this move, so your right arm is in the air and your left arm is out to the side, and shake. Drop your arms to your sides.

The K-Motion. With your feet together, raise your left arm up and out into the high V-shape. Move your right arm across your body so your right hand is level with your left hip. Hold for three, then shake your pom-poms. Now reverse so your right arm is in the air and your left arm crosses your body.

Buckets. Jump your feet apart and bring your arms straight out in front of you with your fists facing down as though you're holding the handle of a bucket in each hand. Hold for three then shake those pom-poms.

The Banana. Jump your feet together. Arch backwards and reach your arms up and behind you. Hold for three, then shake. Straighten up and drop your arms to your sides.

Touchdown. Jump your legs out. Lift both arms straight up above your head, palms facing each other. Hold for a count of three. (This is the move cheerleaders use at football games when their team scores.)

The Knee Drop. Jump down into this final position with your right knee bent in front of you and your left knee on the floor as shown below. Hold your arms out in a high V-shape above your head and give those pom-poms one final shake while you shout out your favourite chant.

Well done, brilliant show!

TEAM TIME

Cheerleading is a team sport, so grab a group of friends and practise a routine that works through all the basic moves one after the other, in the order shown on pages 8 and 9.

Ask someone to count out 1-2-3-4, 1-2-3-4, throughout the routine to make sure you all keep in time with each other.

DRESS RIGHT

Your squad needs to look like a team, so it is important to match your colours and outfits. Your school sports skirt or shorts, with a T-shirt of your chosen colour is a good choice. Get everyone to tie their hair back into high ponytails and secure with ribbons in your team colours. Remember, wear a big smile, even if your team is losing!

ADD A CHANT

Here's a chant to try, but feel free to make up your own.

Two, four, six, eight.
Who do we appreciate?
The cheerleader girls!

Our team to win,
Yours in the bin.

Pom-poms up,
Pom-poms down,
We know our team's
The best in town.

We're the best,
We beat the rest.

HOW TO MAKE YOUR OWN POM-POMS

Cheerleaders hold a pom-pom in each hand – this is a shaggy ball of plastic strips attached to a handle. You can buy these in a toy shop, but it is so much more fun to make your own with recycled plastic carrier bags from the supermarket.

You Will Need:

- six or ten bags per pom-pom, depending how big you want them to be – try to match the bags to your team colours
- a ruler • scissors • a felt-tip pen

WHAT YOU DO

1. Smooth each bag out flat on the floor. Use a ruler and pen to draw a line 30 cm above the base of the bag and parallel to it.

2. Cut along the line, removing the top of the bag along with the handles.

3. Starting at the open end, cut about 20 cm down the depth of the bag, stopping 10 cm from the bottom. Repeat this across the whole width of the bag to form strips that are about 2 cm wide.

4. Repeat the process with all your bags.

5. Gather the prepared bags, holding them at the uncut bases. To make a handle for your pom-pom, scrunch the bases together and secure by wrapping a long strip of sticky tape around them or use a strong elastic band. Finally, rub the finished pom-poms between your hands to fluff them up.

HOW TO MAKE ICE CREAM FROM SNOW

Forget building snowmen. When a flurry of the white stuff starts to fall, it means only one thing – pudding!

You Will Need:

- a cup of full fat milk – icy cold
- ½ a teaspoon of vanilla essence (optional)
- ½ a cup of sugar • four or five cups of CLEAN snow

WHAT YOU DO

1. Collect your snow from outside in a clean bowl.

2. Bring the snow into your house and pop it in the freezer until you need it.

3. Mix together the milk, sugar and vanilla essence and stir until the sugar dissolves in the milk.

4. Slowly add spoonfuls of snow to the mixture. Stir it constantly until it's as thick as normal ice cream.

5. Eat quickly or pop it back in the freezer to ice up.

HOW TO INTERPRET YOUR DOODLES

The doodles you draw when you're daydreaming are an excellent way to discover what sort of person you really are inside. Next time you realise you have been off in a world of your own, covering a page in doodles, take a look at what you have drawn and find out what it all means below.

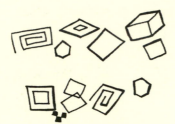

Geometric Shapes
You're a really organised person and the one people turn to when they want to get things done.

Flowers And Curves
You are friendly, understanding and everyone loves you – lucky girl!

A House
You're a homebody who loves to feel safe and secure. You've got everything you want right on your own doorstep.

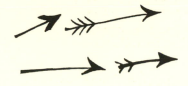

Arrows

You've got big plans for your life and you're determined to reach your goals.

Hearts

You're romantic and emotional. Bet you send loads of cards on Valentine's Day – and get lots in return.

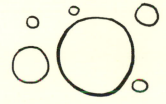

Circles

You enjoy being alone. The trouble is, everyone loves being around you, so you don't often get the chance.

Triangles

You get bored doing the same things every day – you love change and a challenge.

Birds

You're a free spirit who just wants to fly away from it all.

HOW TO MAKE A PEG-DOLL CHRISTMAS ANGEL

Peg dolls have been made by girls just like you for hundreds of years. Here's a peg-doll angel that's easy to make. It would look great decorating a branch of your family's Christmas tree.

You Will Need:

- a round-headed wooden clothes peg
- a felt-tip pen • a pipe cleaner • fabric glue
- some cotton fabric • scissors • a sheet of holographic card • a paper doily • white, yellow or brown wool • glitter and sequins • a ribbon

WHAT YOU DO

1. Draw on your angel's eyes, nose and mouth with felt-tip pens – be as creative as you like.

2. Wind a pipe cleaner around the 'neck' of the peg to make two arms. Bend at each elbow.

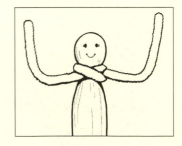

16

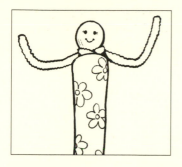

3. Trim a piece of cotton fabric into a rectangle about 8 cm by 5 cm. Squirt some fabric glue along one edge and wrap it around the angel's body just below the arms to form a tube. Use some more glue to fix it into place at the back.

4. Make a cut in the doily from the edge to the centre. Cut a small circle at the centre about the width of your peg. Wrap the doily skirt around the angel and stick in place with fabric glue.

5. Draw the shape of a pair of wings on your holographic card and cut them out. Glue them to the back of your angel.

6. Cut five equal lengths of wool and stick them over the angel's head to form her hair.

7. Add glitter and sequins to give your angel some sparkle.

8. Finally, cut a length of pretty ribbon and tie it around the angel's neck. Tie the two ends of the ribbon in a knot to form a hanging loop.

HOW TO SET UP
A NAIL SALON

Why not set up a nail salon in your bedroom? Invite your friends over and impress them with your professional manicure skills.

TOP TRICKS AT YOUR FINGERTIPS

- File nails into a slightly squared oval. The 'squoval' is the most flattering shape for all nails.

- Don't file too deeply into the sides of nails – this is where most breakages start.

- Keep an old pair of fine nylon tights in your manicure kit. Once you've finished filing a nail, check the tip is ultra-smooth by running it over the tights – it shouldn't snag.

- Apply nail polish to a nail in three broad strokes – one down the side, one down the middle, one down the other side. If you're using a strong colour, two thin coats are better than one thick one.

- Don't use just the tip of the brush to apply polish or you'll apply too much and encourage air bubbles. The bristles should be splayed out horizontally against the nail. This means you'll get thinner, more even layers – and a more professional finish.

- Dry wet nail polish in an instant by plunging your hands into a bowl of ice-cold water.

A QUICK FIX

A good manicurist always has neat nails herself. So make sure you look after your own hands. If you want a manicured look but haven't got time to play around with polish, try pouring a few drops of olive oil onto a clean, soft cloth and buff your nails quickly.

If you've got an extra moment to spare, sweep the tip of a white nail pencil under the top edges of your nails for an instant French Manicure look.

HOW TO MAKE
A BOAT IN A NUTSHELL

If you crack a walnut really carefully the shell will break into two perfect halves. In minutes you can transform them into boats which will float beautifully on water.

Cut a rectangle of paper to create the sail. You can decorate it if you like. Thread a cocktail stick through it to form a mast.

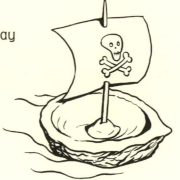

Push a small lump of modelling clay into the middle of the walnut half. Push one end of the cocktail stick into the modelling clay.

Grab a friend and head off to the nearest stream. Launch your boats and see which one sails into the sunset the fastest.

19

HOW TO DEAL WITH SPOTS

As a general rule, spots are best left well alone. However, if you can't resist trying to treat them, remember different spots need different treatment.

RED SPOT

Never try to squeeze a spot that's just a lump without a 'head' on it – if you do, you'll just push the infection deeper and risk scarring your skin.

In the morning, hold an ice cube over the spot for a few seconds to take the swelling down and shrink the spot.

Get to work with the spot cream, antiseptic lotion or a little tea-tree oil at night. The spot will soon start to clear.

YELLOW SPOT

If the spot has come to a head and has a yellow top to it (yuk!), you can try working on it – but very gently.

Make a cup of warm camomile tea and dip some cotton wool into it. Then place the cotton wool onto the spot and hold it there for a minute.

Repeat this several times. Softening the skin like this will help to prevent any bruising and scarring when you start to tackle the spot.

With a paper tissue covering your fingertips, gently apply a LITTLE pressure all around the spot until it deflates. Never use dirty fingers to touch a spot – it could become infected and will look worse and last longer.

If the spot doesn't pop straight away when you apply gentle pressure, stop and try again another day.

Finish off with a dab of tea-tree oil on the affected area.

Important. Never squeeze a spot until it bleeds – this can scar your skin. Never cover a squeezed spot with make-up or cream until it's completely dried out.

HOW TO RECOGNISE YOUR BIRTHSTONE

'Gemstones' are minerals or rocks that can be cut, polished and used in beautiful jewellery. Some gemstones are linked to a particular month of the year – they are known as 'birthstones'. They make a special birthday gift, and some people say it's really lucky to wear your own birthstone.

Month	Birthstone	Colour Of Stone
JANUARY	garnet	dark red
FEBRUARY	amethyst	purple
MARCH	aquamarine	pale blue
APRIL	diamond	white
MAY	emerald	green
JUNE	moonstone	cream

Find out which is your birthstone in the chart below.

If you're not lucky enough to own your own birthstone (unfortunately, lots of them are very expensive), why not paint a stone in the correct colour following the instructions on pages 42 and 43?

Alternatively, try wearing an item of clothing that's the colour of your birthstone. After all, everyone needs a little luck in their lives.

Month	Birthstone	Colour Of Stone
JULY	ruby	red
AUGUST	peridot	pale green
SEPTEMBER	sapphire	deep blue
OCTOBER	pink tourmaline	pink
NOVEMBER	topaz	yellow
DECEMBER	turquoise	sky blue

HOW TO TRAIN YOUR BRAIN

You might not be the best at maths or know all the capital cities of the world, but perhaps you're the most creative person in your family or school. Try this test to find out.

THE PAPERCLIP CHALLENGE

You can use paperclips to do much more than just clipping pieces of paper together. Spend two minutes writing down as many uses for paperclips as you can think of. Be as creative, daring and silly as you like.

Once the two minutes is up, count up your ideas.

4 is the average number of uses people come up with.
8 uses is high.
12 uses is rare.
16 uses – only one person in a thousand thinks up this many.

Why not get your friends and family to try and see who's the most creative?

GETTING STARTED

Here are some ideas to get you going. You could use paperclips …

- … as bookmarks.

- … to scatter on the beach in their hundreds and drive people using metal detectors mad.

- … as a prize in the world's worst raffle.

- … as fish hooks.

- … joined together to make a necklace.

- … as a tiny pair of skis for a budgie.

- … to hold up a fallen hem on your skirt.

- … to unclog a blocked pencil sharpener.

- … for painting tiny dots on a picture.

- … as the anchor of a walnut shell boat (see page 19).

- … as a climbing frame for fleas.

- … as clothes hangers for dolls.

HOW TO GET GUM OUT OF YOUR HAIR

Question: How do you get chewing gum out of your hair?
Do you use … a) an ice cube? b) peanut butter? c) a nit comb?
Answer: All three!

GUM, GOING, GONE

Hold an ice cube over the affected hair. This will make the chewing gum go really hard and cold. When it does, crack it with your fingers and pick off the bits.

Rub any stray remaining bits of gum with peanut butter – this sounds really strange but peanut butter has a magical effect on chewing gum. Massage it in thoroughly.

Comb out the peanut butter with a nit comb (any fine-toothed comb will do at a pinch).

Shampoo and condition your hair afterwards.

Finally, tuck in to some creamy, nutty goodness – you deserve it.

Warning. Don't touch peanut butter or eat it if you have a nut allergy.

HOW TO MAKE
A CRISP-BAG BADGE

Here's how to make a fun badge. Be careful, everyone will want one.

You Will Need:

- a bag of crisps (the small size, not a family bag!)
- a baking tray • oven gloves • a wooden spoon
- a safety pin • sticky tape

WHAT YOU DO

1. Turn the oven on to its hottest setting (ask for adult help and supervision whenever you use the oven).

2. Carefully open the bag of crisps and eat the contents. It is a terrible job, but someone has to do it ...

3. Shake out any crumbs and wipe the inside of the bag clean with a piece of kitchen roll.

4. Place the bag on a baking tray and flatten it out as much as you can.

5. Pop the tray in the oven for around 10 minutes. Check the bag every couple of minutes to make sure it doesn't burn. It should begin to shrink!

6. When the badge has shrunk to about two thirds of its original size and is about 5 cm wide, take the tray out of the oven using the oven gloves.

7. Using the back of a wooden spoon, quickly flatten out any kinks or curls in the mini bag. Then leave it to cool for five minutes.

8. Once the bag is completely cool, pick it up – it will now be much harder and thicker than a normal crisp packet.

9. Secure a safety pin onto the back of the badge with some sticky tape.

10. Pin to your lapel. Stand back and wait for compliments!

HOW TO PLAY SEVENS

Sevens is a great ball game which you can play by yourself or with friends. The moves you have to make get harder the further you progress, so see how long you can keep going.

HOW TO PLAY

Find a tennis ball and a flat wall outside. Stand about two metres from the wall and follow this routine:

- Throw the ball at the wall and catch it.

- Throw the ball at the wall, let it bounce, then catch it.

- Throw the ball at the wall, swat it back at the wall with the palm of your hand, then catch it.

- Throw the ball at the wall, swat it back at the wall, let it bounce once and catch it.

- Throw the ball at the wall, let it bounce once, bounce it again with the palm of your hand and catch it.

- Throw the ball at the wall, swat it back at the wall, let it bounce once, bounce it again with your hand and catch it.

- Throw the ball at the wall, swat it back at the wall, let it bounce, bounce it again, swat it back at the wall and catch it.

AND NOW THE HARD BIT

Add one of the following variations each time you go through the whole routine.

- Clap your hands each time you throw the ball.

- Clap your hands twice after throwing the ball.

- Spin around each time you throw the ball.

- Go through each stage using only your right hand.

- Repeat each stage using just your left hand.

- Start each stage by throwing the ball under your right leg.

- Now try each stage throwing the ball under your left leg.

If all that is just too easy you can combine as many of your own variations as you like. Why not challenge a friend to a Sevens championship match?

HOW TO LOOK BEAUTIFUL TOMORROW

Want to look fab but can't be bothered with lengthy beauty routines? Simple – just boost your looks while you're tucked up in bed. You'll look beautiful in the morning.

Get Prettier Feet. There's no need to scrub away at dry heels and hard skin for hours. Simply slather on lots of thick body lotion, pull on some cotton socks and head for bed. You'll wake up to much softer feet.

Get Smoother Lips. Slick chapped lips with petroleum jelly before bed. In the morning, rub gently with a clean damp flannel to remove any flakes of dead skin.

Get Softer Hands. Apply a dollop of hand cream straight after washing your hands – it'll seal in extra moisture and work wonders on hands and nails while you dream.

Get Shinier Hair. For the glossiest locks ever, just smooth lots of thick conditioner onto freshly shampooed hair before bedtime. Protect your pillow by covering it with an old towel. Rinse and style your hair in the morning.

Get Clearer Skin. Don't worry about that spot ruining your day. Just dot on some tea-tree oil before bed – it's the best pimple buster known to girl-kind.

HOW TO MAKE A HEN EGG COSY

If you can stitch two pieces of fabric together, you can make this gorgeous hen cosy for your boiled egg.

You Will Need:

- brown felt for the body of the hen
- felt in a contrasting colour
for the wings and eyes of the hen
- two lengths of coloured embroidery
thread – any contrasting colour you like
- fabric glue • scissors
- pins • a large needle
- tracing paper • a felt-tip pen

WHAT YOU DO

1. Place the tracing paper over the top of the pattern opposite and draw over the outline of the wing and the outline of the

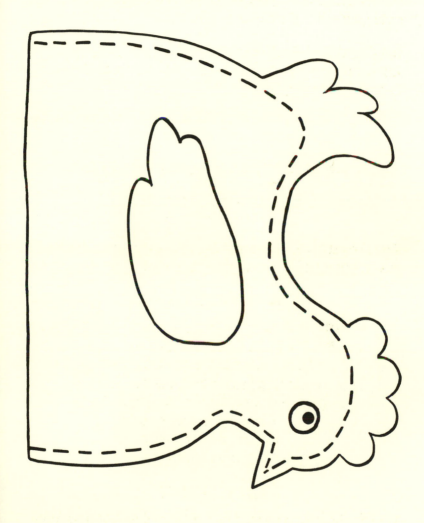

body with a felt-tip pen. Then repeat, so you have two sets of matching pieces – two bodies and two wings.

2. Cut out all the patterns from the paper.

3. Pin the paper patterns to the felt and cut them out.

4. Cut small circles of felt to create the hen's eyes.

5. Thread a needle and make a knot near the end of the thread. Join the two body shapes together using a simple 'tacking stitch' around the edges. Working from right to left, push the needle in and out through both layers of the felt.

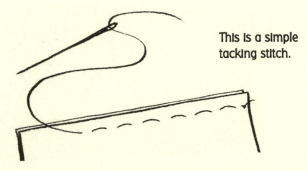

This is a simple tacking stitch.

6. You need to leave the base of the hen open. So when you get to the end, secure the last stitch by going back to the end of the last stitch and bringing the needle through again. Repeat. Snip off the remaining thread.

7. Use the glue to stick on the wings and eye shapes.

8. Pop your hen cosy over an egg sitting in an egg cup. It will look so cute that you will be asked to make one for each member of your family. Soon your breakfast table will look like a hen coop.

HOW TO DRY FLOWERS

Dry the flowers and herbs you pick in the summer and you'll have a bedroom full of blooms all year round.

1. Just pick your flowers – try to choose perfect plants with long stems. Roses and lavender work well.

2. Snip the stems neatly and pick off any leaves from the lower half of the stem.

3. Gather the flowers into small bunches, fastening them together with an elastic band.

4. Open each bunch into a fan shape so the air can get to every bloom.

5. Hang the flowers upside down in a dark, dry place (an airing cupboard is ideal) for two or three weeks.

Display your dry flowers in a pretty vase or container. There is no need to add water.

A bunch of dried flowers makes a perfect gift for Mother's Day.

HOW TO TIDY YOUR ROOM IN 15 MINUTES

Your bedroom might look as though a jumble sale is just about to take place, but you can make it presentable in only 15 minutes. When you see what you can achieve in just a quarter of an hour, you might even resolve to get really organised ...

BEFORE YOU START

Put on some of your favourite music. If it has a great beat and you can sing along to it, the job will seem much more fun.

Grab yourself a couple of bin liners, a tray and a couple of empty boxes. You'll also need a damp cloth and a vacuum cleaner ready. Pull back the curtains and roll up the blinds. Open the windows to let some clean fresh air in while you tidy.

HERE WE GO

Why not get someone to time you?

15 Minutes To Go. Sweep all the stray clothes from around the room and dump them on the bed. Sort through them, putting dirty clothes into a laundry bag ready for washing – remove this from the room. Put away the rest of your clothes in wardrobes and drawers, making sure they're properly shut afterwards.

12 Minutes To Go. Gather items that don't belong in your room (like dirty dishes and things you have borrowed from your mum) and put them on a tray. Put the tray outside your bedroom door to be sorted later.

11 Minutes To Go. Gather up everything that can be thrown away from the floor and all visible surfaces. Dump it all in a bin bag – you can sort out rubbish for recycling later on. Remove the bag from the room.

9 Minutes To Go. Spend one minute gathering all stray DVDs, CDs, games and stuffed animals together and putting them back where they live. Do the most you can in the time.

8 Minutes To Go. Spend one minute tidying away books and shuffling papers into neat piles. Again, do as much as you can in the time.

7 Minutes To Go. There's no time for thorough filing or sorting today. Gather together all remaining stray items (like photographs, magazines, odd socks) that are lying around and dump them into an empty box – it's better than stuffing it all under the bed. Pop them in the corner of the room or under a table out of sight. Once it's all together you may feel inspired to tackle it.

5 Minutes To Go. Get a damp cloth and wipe any dusty surfaces.

3 Minutes To Go. Make your bed, taking care to straighten out the duvet and plump up the pillows.

2 Minutes To Go. Vacuum the floor. Do the main part of the floor first, finishing with the corners and edges of the room if you've got time.

Finished. Well done – you did a great job. Now how about the living room?

HOW TO HAVE THE SHINIEST SHOES EVER

A mirror-like sheen on your leather shoes takes a little know-how and a lot of elbow grease, but it's worth a go.

1. Take out any laces and undo any straps.

2. Wipe off all excess dirt from the surface of your shoes with a damp cloth.

3. Remove any ingrained dirt or stains with saddle soap – this is available from shoe repair shops. Rub a little bit of saddle soap into the shoe with a damp cloth. Then keep rubbing until the leather looks really clean.

4. Buff your shoes with a clean, dry cloth.

5. Use an old cotton T-shirt to apply some shoe polish. Unlike a brush, a T-shirt won't scratch the leather. Dab a small amount of polish onto the T-shirt and rub it into the leather in small circles. Keep going until you see a shine start to appear. Continue over the whole shoe.

6. Leave your shoes on a piece of newspaper while the polish dries fully.

7. Grab a clean cotton cloth and buff the leather to a final shine.

Voilà – beautiful shiny shoes.

HOW TO PLAY CLOCK PATIENCE

Here is a game of Patience played in a clock pattern. It's a perfect way to while away a wet afternoon.

HOW TO PLAY

Deal 12 cards face-down in a pattern like the numbers on a clock face. Put another card in the centre of your 'clock'. Repeat this until you have four cards in each pile.

Turn over the top card on the centre pile. This card directs you to one of the piles on the clock face. Aces go at one o'clock, twos at two o'clock, right round to the Queens at twelve o'clock. Place your card under the pile or beside it, then turn over the top card of this pile to find out where to go to next.

Whenever you turn over a King, you must place it in the centre of the clock and take a card from the centre pile to start again.

The aim is to turn over the cards in all 12 piles – but once you have revealed all four Kings the game is over.

HOW TO EAT A GOLDFISH

Don't panic, you don't really have to eat a goldfish. This is a great trick and is bound to cause quite a stir whenever you perform it. All you need is a goldfish bowl filled with water containing a thin slice of carrot cut into the shape of a goldfish.

WHAT YOU DO

1. Stand between your friend and the bowl. Discreetly turn away from her and swirl the water in the bowl with your fingers. This will make the carrot 'goldfish' appear to swim.

2. Turn back and announce you're feeling peckish. Your pal may suggest a biscuit or a piece of fruit. Refuse politely, telling her you have a perfect high-protein snack to hand.

3. Plunge your hand into the bowl and pull out the 'fish'. Bounce it around in your palm a bit to make it look as though it's flapping around.

4. Pop the carrot into your mouth, crunch it, and swallow. Smile sweetly and leave the room, while your friend opens and closes her mouth in horror, looking a bit like ... well, a goldfish!

HOW TO MAKE A FRIENDSHIP STONE

A friendship stone is a really special gift to give your best friend. She can proudly display it on her bedroom windowsill or use it as a paperweight on her desk.

You Will Need:

- a pebble • some paints • paint brushes
- felt-tip pens • water-based acrylic varnish

WHAT YOU DO

1. Wash and dry the pebble before you begin.

2. Paint on a design. You can choose any design you like – adding your friend's initials would look good. Leave it to dry.

3. Use the pens (or paint) to write on the underside of the stone. This could be your friend's name or a message like 'best friends forever'.

4. Paint on a coat of varnish to seal in your design and words forever.

5. Wait for the stone to dry completely, then give it to your pal.

Top Tip. You're not allowed to remove stones from certain beaches – so always check first. Garden centres sell bags of stones in various shapes and sizes. You may even find the perfect stone in the park, your garden or in a friend's garden.

HOW TO CATCH A SPIDER

If you'd rather not share your room with a spider, don't be tempted to squash it. Instead, check out how to capture it for long enough to transfer it elsewhere.

- If the spider's loitering on a wall or windowsill, just place a clear glass tumbler over the top. Slide a piece of stiff card under the rim. You can now carry the spider safely out to the garden and release it.

- If the spider has spun a web, you'll need to hold the glass underneath – spiders tend to drop down from their webs when they sense danger. Again, seal it inside the glass with a piece of card.

- If a spider's crawling high up a wall or a ceiling, try catching it on a feather duster. Once you've caught it, tip it into a glass and seal with card.

HOW TO KNOW WHICH COLOURS TO WEAR

The secret to finding clothes that suit you is to decide whether your colouring is 'WARM' or 'COOL'. This mini questionnaire will help you find out.

WHAT COLOUR ARE YOUR EYES?

Take a mirror over to the window when the daylight is good and have a good look at the colour of your eyes. Are they ...

a. ... golden brown, green, green-blue, turquoise, hazel with gold or brown flecks?

b. ... deep brown or black-brown, grey-blue or dark blue, hazel with white, grey or blue flecks?

WHAT IS YOUR SKIN TONE?

Go back to the mirror and check out the colour of your skin –
pay particular attention to the skin along your jawline. Is it ...

a. ... brown with pink or golden undertones, pale with peach or
gold undertones, freckled, golden brown?

b. ... very dark brown, olive, pale or medium with faint pink
undertones or no colour in cheeks?

WHAT IS YOUR HAIR COLOUR?

Now take a look at your hair colour. Is it ...

a. ... deep brown with gold or red highlights, red or strawberry
blonde?

b. ... blue-black, deep coffee brown, medium ash brown,
medium golden brown, ash blonde, golden blonde?

ARE YOU WARM OR COOL?

You'll have answered mostly 'a's or 'b's.

If you are mostly an 'a's girl your colouring is WARM. You will
look great in 'Earth Tones'. This means golden browns,
yellows, orange-based reds, rich pinks and rich greens.

If your answers were mostly 'b's your colouring is COOL. You
will look great in 'Jewel Tones'. This means blues, clear greens,
bright pinks, purples and blue-based reds.

HOW TO LIVEN UP A SLEEPOVER

Here are two games that will add some laughter to any sleepover and are perfect for four or more friends to play together.

THE RING GAME

All you need for this game is a long piece of string (about three metres) and a ring. Slide the ring onto the string, then tie the ends of the string together to create a giant loop.

Choose one player to stand in the middle of the string circle. The other players stand in a circle around this person, holding the string in their hands.

The player in the middle closes their eyes and counts to ten. Meanwhile, the other players pass the ring along the string, hiding it in their hands.

When the player in the middle has finished counting, she opens her eyes and has to try and guess where the ring is. While she is trying to guess, the other players can carry on passing the ring from person to person – feel free to pretend you're passing the ring even when you're not.

When the player in the middle eventually guesses correctly, she changes places with the person who was caught with the ring in her hand.

Play starts again.

THE KNIFE AND FORK GAME

This is possibly the best game in the world because it gives you the perfect excuse to eat chocolate.

Sit on the floor in a circle. Put a large, no, a HUGE bar of wrapped chocolate on a plate in the middle, with a knife and fork on either side, a pair of gloves, a hat and a scarf.

Starting with the youngest player, take it in turns to roll a dice. As soon as someone throws a six, she must put on the hat, scarf and gloves, grab a knife and fork and start to eat the chocolate. The problem is she is not allowed to touch the chocolate with her hands and must use the knife and fork to get through the wrapper and lift the chocolate into her mouth.

While this is going on, the other players continue to take turns rolling the dice as quickly as they can. As soon as another six is thrown, the player eating the chocolate must stop and give the knife, fork, hat, gloves and scarf to the person who threw the six, who puts them on and gets munching.

Play continues until the chocolate is all gone.

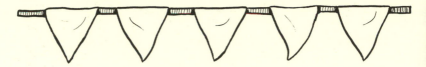

HOW TO MAKE COOL BUNTING FOR YOUR BEDROOM

Strings of fabric bunting will transform a boring bedroom into a beautiful boudoir. It can be very expensive in the shops, but you can make your own very cheaply.

You Will Need:

- scraps of cotton fabric
- a length of ribbon at least 2 cm wide by 3 m long
- scissors (ideally use 'pinking sheers' – these are special scissors which have zigzag blades instead of straight ones)
- some fabric glue • a piece of sturdy card
- a ruler • a pencil
- a felt-tip pen

WHAT YOU DO

1. Gather your scraps of cotton fabric – you don't need to buy these, just get permission to cut up some old clothes, sheets or even a tablecloth. Go for any pattern or colour combination you like – though a mix of pretty florals and gingham checks always look great.

2. Draw a triangle on a piece of card using the ruler and

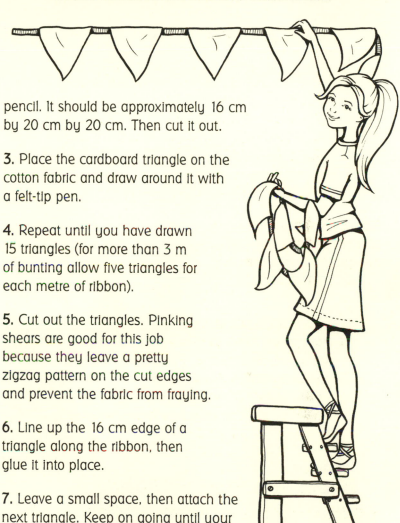

pencil. It should be approximately 16 cm by 20 cm by 20 cm. Then cut it out.

3. Place the cardboard triangle on the cotton fabric and draw around it with a felt-tip pen.

4. Repeat until you have drawn 15 triangles (for more than 3 m of bunting allow five triangles for each metre of ribbon).

5. Cut out the triangles. Pinking shears are good for this job because they leave a pretty zigzag pattern on the cut edges and prevent the fabric from fraying.

6. Line up the 16 cm edge of a triangle along the ribbon, then glue it into place.

7. Leave a small space, then attach the next triangle. Keep on going until your bunting is complete. Leave a little ribbon clear at each end for tying up your bunting.

8. Allow the glue to dry thoroughly before hanging up the bunting in your bedroom.

HOW TO BE AN EGYPTIAN QUEEN

Egyptian queens are said to have been beautiful and clever, but most of all they were incredibly powerful, because people believed they were goddesses. They certainly knew all about 'girl power' thousands of years ago.

Here is how to make sure your friends and family recognise that, deep down, you are an Egyptian queen, too.

ROYAL TREATMENT

- Avoid the risk of being poisoned by rival royals, who are eager to get their hands on your crown. Get a slave to taste your food before you eat anything (a younger brother is ideal). Tell the person who cooked your food that you don't mean to be rude but you can't risk it.

- Insist on writing all your homework in hieroglyphs on rolls of papyrus (the stuff ancient Egyptians used to write on). It will take time, but your history teacher will be seriously impressed.

- Request a pet goose for your next birthday – failing that, a black cat will do.

- Arrange all your possessions in a pyramid shape in the middle of your bedroom.

- Float around in a white tunic, strappy sandals and dozens of bracelets. The bad news is that Egypt's the most powerful female pharaoh, Hatshepsut, wore a false beard – not the best look to try and carry off.

- Wear lots and lots of make-up – especially heavy black eyeliner and green eyeshadow. When applying the eyeliner, use the picture below for inspiration.

- Egyptian queens often had to marry their brothers, but this is one tradition you might want to ignore!

- Insist your parents build an obelisk in the garden – this is a tall, narrow, stone monument with a pyramid shape at the top.

- Demand that four friends pick up your chair and carry you when you pop to the shops.

- If your mum's snoozing in front of the TV, wrap her in bandages from top to toe – she is the Queen Mummy after all. It is probably not a good idea to remove her internal organs and put them in a canopic jar – she might get cross.

HOW TO MAKE YOUR OWN PICK-AND-MIX SWEETS

There's no need to head to the sweet shop when you can make your very own pick-and-mix sweets. They make wonderful gifts for friends and family.

COCONUT ICE

Here's a simple way to make this tasty coconutty treat.

You Will Need:

- 350 g desiccated coconut • 350 g icing sugar
- 400 g tin of condensed milk
- ½ teaspoon of pink food colouring
- a bowl • a sieve • a loaf tin • some plastic wrap

WHAT YOU DO

1. Pour the condensed milk into a large bowl. Sift in the icing sugar by putting it in a sieve and tapping the side of the sieve with your hand.

2. Add the desiccated coconut and stir until there are no dry bits of coconut left.

3. Line a loaf tin with some plastic wrap and spread half the mixture in the bottom.

4. Add the pink colouring to the mixture left in the bowl and stir until it is an even colour all the way through.

5. Spread the pink mixture on top of the white in the loaf tin and then place in the refrigerator overnight to set.

6. When the mixture has set, remove it from the loaf tin and cut up into squares.

PEPPERMINT CREAMS

Delicious and full of minty flavour, peppermint creams make the perfect pick-and-mix partners for your coconut ice.

You Will Need:

- 1 egg white • 450 g icing sugar
- 100 g plain or milk chocolate
- ½ teaspoon of peppermint flavouring
- ½ teaspoon of green food colouring
- a glass bowl • a pan • a baking tray covered with foil

WHAT YOU DO

1. Get an adult to help you separate the egg white from the yoke. Pour it into a mixing bowl with the peppermint flavouring and green food colouring. Mix well.

2. Now sift in the icing sugar and stir until the ingredients combine to form a smooth ball – add some more icing sugar if the mixture is a bit sticky.

3. Dust your work surface with a little more sugar and roll the mixture into a long sausage shape about the thickness of a pound coin.

4. Slice into discs about ½ cm thick and place on a board to dry.

5. Melt the chocolate. You can do this by breaking it into squares and placing them in a glass bowl. Place the bowl over a pan of barely simmering water and stir until they've melted – ask an adult to help you with this.

6. Dip one side of each peppermint cream into the melted chocolate. Place each sweet onto a foil-covered tray to set.

HOW TO PUT ON A SHOEBOX-THEATRE SHOW

Thrill your family and friends with a show all about them.

THE THEATRE

Start by making your theatre out of an old shoebox – shoe shops often have some to spare if you don't have one at home.

1. Stand the shoebox on one of its long sides and cut an opening at each of the short ends. These openings are where your 'actors' will enter the stage.

2. Decide where your play is going to be set, such as in a house, a school or by the seaside. Make a scenery backdrop for your theatre by cutting a sheet of paper that will fit snugly into the base of the shoebox. Then you can either draw the scenery or use magazine pictures. You could even use family photographs cut out and stuck to the paper, but ask first.

3. Add any extra bits to your 'set' that you like – perhaps some cardboard trees, dolls' house furniture or fancy felt flooring.

4. Use two thin pieces of fabric (each two thirds of the width of your stage) to create a pair of curtains at the front of the theatre. Make two holes either side of the stage, just beneath the roof. Tie a piece of string between the holes.

Fold the top of each piece of fabric over the string and then secure it with a simple tacking stitch (see page 34) about a finger's width below the string. Check that your curtains open and close.

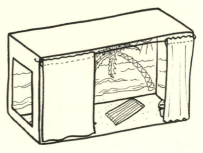

THE CAST

Cut out the faces of your family and friends from old photographs (always ask permission first). Stick them onto bodies cut from the cardboard of the shoebox lid. With felt-tip pens, draw costumes on the bodies.

Use sticky tape to attach your 'actors' to straws or sticks – one end of the stick should be stuck sideways across the back of the body, so you can use the stick 'handle' to move the actor from the sides of the stage. Remember that some characters will want to come in on the right-hand side of the stage and some from the left, so attach the handles accordingly.

Top Tip. You'll need a friend or two to help you if you're going to have more than two characters on stage at any one time.

WRITE YOUR SHOW

Write a simple script that's based on a real event in your characters' lives. Perhaps it's a birthday party, a day on the beach or something funny that happened in school. If you don't want to write it down, spend a few minutes thinking about your story before you begin.

TOP WRITERS' TIPS

- Use people's real nicknames.

- If someone, like your dad, has a favourite saying, include that as well – everyone will recognise it and they will laugh.

- Try to include a few jokes.

- Keep your story really simple with a beginning, middle and an end.

- Think about including a song and dance at the end – it's always a crowd-pleaser.

HOW TO REMOVE A RING THAT'S STUCK

Have you ever tried on a friend's ring that's too small and got it stuck? If it happens again, don't panic – just follow these steps.

Step One: Cool It. Fill a bowl with cold water and tip in a tray of ice. Hold your hand in the ice water for ten seconds (or as long as you can bear to). This will help take down any swelling in your finger.

Step Two: Oil It. Rub plenty of hand cream, olive oil or washing-up liquid in and around the ring and up the length of your finger.

Step Three: Twist It. Gently twist (not yank) the ring, as you slowly work it up and over the knuckle of your finger.

HOW TO SALUTE THE SUN

If you've never tried yoga, this is a great place to start. The sun salutation is a series of 12 yoga exercises to stretch your body, calm your mind and really set you up for the day.

These moves should all flow naturally from one to another, so make sure you do them all in the right order.

Take your time and keep practising. Make sure you stretch gently and only stretch as far as is comfortable. However, if any of the movements hurt it is a good idea to stop straight away.

THE SUN SALUTATION

1. Stand with your feet together, hands in front of your chest as though you're praying. Breathe in gently and raise your arms.

2. Bend backwards, raising your arms to the sky, palms facing up, allowing your eyes to look up and back. You should only bend back as far as is comfortable.

3. Breathe out and bend forward as far as you can – keeping your knees straight (don't worry if you can't touch your toes).

4. Breathe in and step your right leg back, resting the knee on the floor. Look forward.

5. Bring your left leg back to join your right leg. Support your body on your hands and your toes if you can. This is called the 'Plank Pose'.

6. Breathe out as you lower your knees, chest and forehead to the ground. Keep your elbows in at your sides as your arms bend.

7. Breathing in, arch your back and stretch your head and neck upwards. This is called the 'Cobra Pose'.

8. Breathe out, straighten your arms, and push yourself back so your bottom is in the air and your legs are straight. This is known as the 'Downward Dog'.

9. Breathe in as you bend your right leg, bringing it forward and placing it between your hands.

10. Breathing out, bring your left foot next to your right foot. Straighten your legs and bend forward with knees locked and touch the floor next to your feet.

11. As you breathe in, reach your arms forward, and then gently bend backwards. Keep your arms close to your ears.

12. Breathe out and return to the very first position, gradually bringing your arms down. Finish with your hands in front of you in the prayer position.

HOW TO MAKE
AN APRIL FOOL MEAL

April 1st, otherwise known as April Fool's day, is a great day to play practical jokes on your family and friends. Tricks with food are always a real winner.

Here are some ideas to turn mealtime into trick-time. Make sure you prepare them well in advance. Invite your guests to your April Fool meal, then sit back and watch the fun.

FOOD FUN

- If your milk comes in cartons, turn it blue with a few drops of food colouring. No one will notice until they pour it out.

- If your family eats O-shaped cereal, thread them all onto a piece of string and put them back in the box.

- Make a fake 'fried egg'. Arrange a spoonful of natural yogurt in an oval on a plate. Pop an apricot half in the middle. Serve it up to your family with a rasher of real bacon.

- Make some jelly following the instructions on the packet. Before it sets, pour the jelly into glasses. Pop a straw into each one and put in the fridge. Wait until the jelly sets before you serve your 'fruit squash'. Watch your guests try to drink it!

- Put an empty eggshell upside down in an egg cup and surprise someone with a boiled egg that's got nothing inside.

- Scoop a small hole in an apple with the end of a spoon and insert a sweet gummy worm – yuck!

- Serve a scoop of mashed potato in an ice cream cone – tell your guests it's vanilla-flavoured ice cream.

- With a pin, pierce several holes in a drinking straw, then pop it in a glass of squash.

- Put plastic wrap over the top of a glass of milk, and watch the confusion as someone puts it to their lips.

- Swap the sugar and salt over.

- Scrape the butter icing out from the middle of a biscuit and replace it with toothpaste.

Top Tip. Some people say that on April 1st you only have until midday to make your April Fool. If you play a practical joke after midday the joke's on you. Other people say it's fine to play tricks all day long.

HOW TO PRETEND YOU ARE A SURFER GIRL

It's easy to convince people you're a surfer girl without ever setting foot in the water. There are two main areas to perfect – you need to get the look and talk the talk.

LOOK RIGHT

Surfer girls dress cool and casual – it's about looking relaxed and sporty, rather than dressing up to impress boys.

- Base your look around shorts and a bikini top. Add a few layers of faded T-shirts (ones with sailor stripes or seaside images are particularly great). Top off with a colourful hoodie.

- Flip-flops and loads of friendship bracelets are essential.

- Consider borrowing a wetsuit and having it draped casually over your shoulders so it looks as though you are going to hit the beach later.

Top Tip. Surfer girls' hair always looks beautifully 'tousled' or rumpled by the sun, sea and sand. Get the effect by mixing two tablespoons of salt in half a litre of warm water. Pour it over your hair after shampooing and don't rinse it out. This salty rinse will give your hair an authentic beach-babe look.

TALK RIGHT

Learn some essential 'surf speak'. As you grow in confidence, try dropping a few of the following phrases into your conversation to convince people you're a bona fide surfer girl.

The Deck. The bit of the surfboard you stand on.

Quiver. A surfer's collection of surfboards.

Carve A Wave. This is the classic surfing move where you make wiggly turns when you are surfing on a wave.

Impact Zone. The place where the waves are breaking.

The Soup. The white foamy water created when a wave has broken.

Dropping In. Sneaking onto a wave that's already occupied by another surfer – the quickest way to make a surfer angry with you.

Stink Eye. A mean stare normally given when another surfer's done something bad, like dropping in to your wave.

Tube. This is when a wave breaks over the top of you so you're surfing inside a cylindrical hole – all surfers dream about it.

Green Room. The inside of a tube.

Rip Tide. A really strong current under the water.

Wipeout. This is where you fall off your surfboard in spectacular style!

Grommet. A young surfer.

HOW TO MAKE PAPER SNOWFLAKES

Paper snowflakes are easy-peasy to make and look really good. You can stick them on windows, hang them from the ceiling or stick them on your front door in a circle shape to create a Christmas wreath.

You Will Need:

- some plain white or holographic paper (a square 20 cm by 20 cm for a large snowflake and 10 cm by 10 cm for a smaller one) • a pencil • scissors

HOW TO DO IT

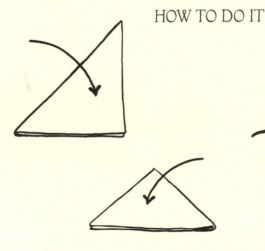

1. Fold the paper in half diagonally. Then fold it in half diagonally again.

2. Now fold one point two thirds of the way across the base of your triangle to achieve the shape shown above.

3. Fold the other point across as shown here.

4. Cut off the two points along this line.

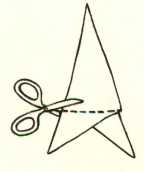

5. Using a pencil, draw zigzags along the long sides of the triangle shape. The more zigzags you draw, the more delicate and decorative your snowflake will be. Use scissors to cut along your pencil lines.

6. Unfold your snowflake and admire the finished result!

Top Tip. If you used plain white paper to make your snowflake, add extra sparkle with some glue and glitter.

HOW TO PLAY WINK MURDER

Wink Murder is the perfect spooky game for a Halloween party.

HOW TO PLAY

Grab at least four friends and sit in a circle. Deal one playing card face down for each person who is playing – one of the cards must be the Ace of Spades.

Each player looks at their card (without showing it to anyone else). The person who has the Ace of Spades is the Murderer!

The players sit in silence, looking at each other. The Murderer kills a victim by winking at her without anyone else noticing. When a player has been winked at she must 'die'. She can scream dramatically or just fall to the floor – so long as she makes it clear to the other players that she is dead.

The Murderer wins if she 'kills' all the other players. She loses if someone spots her and correctly accuses her of being the Murderer before everyone is 'dead'.

HOW TO THROW A SURPRISE PARTY

If you want to make one of your friends happy and shocked at the same time, throw a surprise party for their next birthday. There's more to organising a surprise party than blowing up a few balloons. Here are ten golden rules to follow.

TEN GOLDEN RULES

Rule One. Decide the date. It's important to know that your guest of honour will be available, so check with her family and friends first that she isn't doing something else that day.

Rule Two. Decide on a fake activity that your guest of honour will believe you are doing together on the day. This will put her off the scent.

Rule Three. Send out invitations which make it very clear the party is to be a surprise. You can't emphasise this enough to people. Invite them to come half an hour before the star guest.

Rule Four. If you see or speak to the guest of honour on the big day, be really offhand with her and ignore the fact it's her birthday. Even if she mentions it's her birthday, act disinterested – she'll be hurt, but it'll make the surprise even better later on.

Rule Five. Get the music, food and drinks ready, making sure they're the guest of honour's favourites.

Rule Six. If the guest of honour is someone who lives in your house, make sure you hide all evidence of the party from them.

Rule Seven. When the other guests arrive, store all their shoes, bags and coats out of view so it isn't obvious anyone is at your house.

Rule Eight. Make sure you choose one friend to act as a lookout. She should give a signal to warn all your guests to be quiet when the guest of honour arrives outside the house.

Rule Nine. Switch off all the lights so your guest arrives to an empty-looking, dark house.

Rule Ten. When your guest of honour walks in, switch on the lights and the music, and get everyone to shout 'SURPRISE!' Pick her up off the floor and let the party begin!

HOW TO WRAP A PRESENT BEAUTIFULLY

The only thing more exciting than unwrapping a present is unwrapping a present that looks totally gorgeous. Here are some simple dos and don'ts on how to up the 'Oooh' factor.

DO work on a large, flat, clear area. If it's the floor, sweep it first – little bits of grit can easily tear wrapping paper.

DON'T use too much paper – it'll be difficult to make neat folds when wrapping.

DO place the present in the middle of the sheet of wrapping paper – it'll help you create evenly-sized folds at either end of the gift.

DON'T struggle to wrap paper around an awkwardly-shaped present – putting it in a box first will make it easier to wrap.

DO tear several bits of sticky tape off the roll before you start. Stick one end of them to a smooth, hard object, such as the edge of a table, so that you can just reach for one easily when you need it.

DON'T forget to wrap the paper tightly around your gift and make sharp creases where you fold it.

DO use a heavy object such as a paperweight or a can of beans to keep the flaps in place before you tape them.

DON'T use ordinary ribbon if you want to create a bow. Use the wire-edged sort instead – it holds the shape of the bow brilliantly.

DO attach a tag which says the gift is from you – there's nothing worse than giving someone a great gift and not getting the credit for it!

GET CRAFTY AND CREATIVE

Once you've got the basics right, you can get really creative and wrap pressies in a truly individual way.

• Think beyond ordinary wrapping paper. You could use cartoon pages from a comic, musical scores, maps or posters. Why not try to match the style of paper to the interests of the person who is receiving the gift?

• Decorate plain wrapping paper by painting it with food colouring. This works much better than ordinary poster paints as it doesn't flake when the paper is folded.

• Presents look great when wrapped in a piece of pretty fabric and tied with a ribbon.

• Why not brighten up plain paper by adding sparkly stickers, or dab on some PVA glue and sprinkle it with glitter or confetti. Pasting on feathers works well, too.

• Brown paper and string always looks sophisticated wrapped neatly around a present. You could use a luggage label for the gift tag.

• Turn a small gift into a giant Christmas cracker by stuffing the gift into a paper tube (the one on the inside of a kitchen roll is ideal). Wrap the tube with brightly-coloured tissue paper and tie off the ends with ribbon or elastic bands to resemble a cracker. Decorate with stickers.

HOW TO TELL A HAIRDRESSER WHAT YOU REALLY WANT

Most hairdressers are better at cutting hair than reading minds. So the next time you have your heart set on a new look, remember these golden rules.

PICTURE PERFECT

Don't be shy about tearing pictures out of magazines to show your hairdresser how you want your hair – it'll give you a really good starting point for discussion. If you can't find a picture of what you want, take pictures of what you really don't want. This sounds strange, but it is helpful to show the stylist your dislikes as well as your likes.

SHOW, DON'T TELL

Use your fingers to show exactly how long or short you want your hair to be. That will help prevent the hairdresser cutting a chunk off the bottom of your hair when all you really wanted was the slightest trim.

DON'T USE 'HAIRDRESSER SPEAK'

Do you really know the difference between 'layering' and 'graduating', 'thinning' and 'feathering'? If you use a term incorrectly, the hairdresser may go ahead and give you something completely different to what you had in mind. Describe what you want with simple words and gestures, so you can be sure you get the look you want.

HOW TO MAKE A CORK HORSE

These cute little cork horses look great on a bedroom windowsill. They're so easy to construct, you might be tempted to make a whole herd.

You Will Need:

• a cork • a craft knife • a piece of sturdy card
• a felt-tip pen • scissors • PVA glue
• four cocktail sticks • wool

WHAT YOU DO

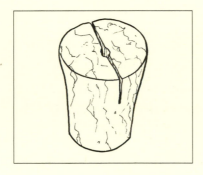

1. The cork will form the horse's body. Make a slit with a sharp craft knife in one end, ready for the head. (Ask an adult for help with this.)

2. Carefully draw a horse's head and neck in profile on the card. Cut it out. Colour in both sides of the card, adding as much horsy detail as you like.

3. Dab some glue onto the end of the neck and slide it into the slit in the cork.

4. Use the four cocktail sticks to form the legs. Push them into the cork body, taking care to get them nicely balanced so your horse stands up straight.

5. Cut some lengths of wool and glue them onto the horse to form a mane and tail.

Top Tip. Why not turn your horse into a zebra by drawing black stripes onto the cork and using black and white wool?

HOW TO EAT YOUR 'FIVE-A-DAY'

If you want to stay healthy on the inside and gorgeous on the outside, you need to eat at least five portions of fruit and veg a day – two servings of fruit and three of vegetables is a great place to start. If you're one of those people who claim not to like fruit and veg, here's how to sneak them into your diet.

- Freeze fruit smoothies to make yummy ice lollies.

- Thread pieces of fruit onto a wooden skewer to make a vitamin-packed 'kebab'. Dip it into yogurt or chocolate sauce.

- Scatter loads of finely chopped veggies on top of your favourite shop-bought pizza before it goes in the oven.

- Sip a carton of fresh fruit juice at lunch, not a fizzy drink.

- Dip raw chunks of vegetables – carrot, celery and cauliflower – into your favourite tasty dips, instead of crisps.

- Tip a handful of fresh or frozen fruit over your ice cream.

- Scatter dried banana chips into your morning cereal.

- Why not try 'ants on a log'? Spread cream cheese on the inside of a stick of celery then sprinkle with raisins.

- Skewer grapes, pineapple and cheese onto cocktail sticks for a perfect party treat.

- Try a new fruit or vegetable! Persuade your parents to buy one piece of exotic fruit you've never tried each week.

HOW TO GROW AN APPLE TREE FROM A SEED

1. Eat your apple and carefully extract the pips.

2. Fill a plant pot with some compost – an old food container will do fine if you haven't got a plant pot.

3. Push several pips into the compost, making sure the soil covers them. Water well.

4. Cover the top of the pot with a loose-fitting lid and leave it in a nice warm place for several weeks. Water from time to time to make sure the compost doesn't dry out.

5. Once your pips start to sprout into shoots, identify the strongest-looking one and pick out the rest.

6. Keep the shoot watered and in a sunny spot and watch it grow. You can use nail scissors to trim your tree and keep it small.

HOW TO SURVIVE A CHARGING ELEPHANT

If you're unfortunate enough to come face to face with an angry elephant, it's useful to know what to do.

EMERGENCY TACTICS

- Always stay 'downwind' of the elephant. To do this you must work out the direction the wind is blowing. You want the wind to be blowing past the elephant towards you, as this will make it harder for the elephant to pick up your scent. Lick your finger and hold it in the air to work out the direction of the wind.

- Learn to recognise the difference between an elephant who is making a 'mock charge' and one who is serious about chasing you. Unfortunately, the art of reading elephants' body language can take many years to perfect and you may get squashed before you learn it. If the elephant's ears are relaxed, it is probably only pretending to charge and if you stay very

still it will lose interest in you. However, if the elephant fans out its ears and shakes them, the charge is probably for real and it is time to skidaddle ... NOW!

• If you have to run for it try moving in sharp zigzags – elephants find it hard to change direction quickly thanks to their huge bulk.

• Don't think that setting a mouse on the elephant will make him run away – elephants are not really frightened of rodents.

• Don't be tempted to jump into water to escape him – elephants are good swimmers. Climb a tree instead – you won't be surprised to hear they're not good at climbing trees. First check the tree for leopards, though.

• If you're running for it and the elephant is getting closer, throw a decoy for it to attack – your jacket or a large branch will do, but a huge sack of peanuts would come in handy here.

HOW TO MAKE YOUR OWN HERBAL TEA

Fresh or dried herbs can be used to make a cup of delicious herbal tea – just add water!

You can pick fresh herbs from the garden, grow them on a windowsill or buy them in bunches or use dried from the supermarket. You will need a teaspoon of dried herbs or three teaspoons of roughly-chopped fresh herbs for one cup of tea. Mint works really well and is particularly easy to grow.

MAKING MINT TEA

1. Pop three teaspoons of roughly chopped mint leaves in a teapot, a jug or a special coffee pot that has a plunger. Pour freshly boiled water over the leaves (ask an adult for help).

2. Leave to 'infuse' for five minutes before you strain and serve the tea.

If you don't like having little bits of leaf floating in your tea, why not make your own herbal teabags?

DIY HERBAL TEA BAGS

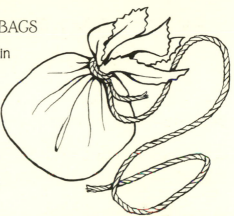

Cut a little square of muslin
– measuring 10 cm by
10 cm. Place your herbs
in the middle, then
gather up the edges.
Tie tightly with string,
leaving the ends long
enough to let you dangle
the teabag in a cup.

HEALING HERBS

Herbs taste delicious, and many have healing properties, too.
However, don't just use any old herbs – it's important to check
they're safe to use first. The two best ones to try first are
peppermint and camomile.

Peppermint. As well as tasting fresh and delicious, peppermint
tea can help soothe a tummy ache and might make you
breathe a little more easily when you have a cold.

Camomile. This herb has a lovely taste, and makes a great
bedtime tea as it's said to help you sleep.

SUN TEA

How about treating yourself to a cup of Sun Tea on a hot day?

Simply fill a clean jar with cold water, throw in a handful of
your favourite crushed fresh herbs, and leave it in the sun for
three or four hours. Stir in a little honey to sweeten, pour over
ice and enjoy. Delicious!

HOW TO MAKE THE PERFECT DAISY CHAIN

There's no nicer way to while away a summer afternoon in the park than by making daisy chains. You can create necklaces or bracelets, crowns or leis, ankle chains or rings. Whatever you go for, make sure yours are the prettiest with these top tips.

PERFECT CHAINS

1. Pick your daisies – select ones with long, strong stalks. Pick them close to the root so you have plenty of stem to work with.

2. Use your thumbnail to split the stalk lengthways – create a slit that's around 1 cm long and about a ½ cm from the end.

3. Thread the stalk of a second daisy through the slit you've created and pull all the way through up to the flower head.

4. Make a slit in the stalk of the second daisy, and repeat. Keep going until your daisy chain is as long as you need it.

5. When you're ready to finish, make a long slit in the stalk of your final daisy and fit the entire head of your first flower through it. Pull gently to tighten.

TOP DAISY TIPS

• You can dry daisy chains by hanging them in a warm place at home such as the airing cupboard.

• Don't limit yourself to daisies – buttercups and poppies work well, too. (Only pick wild flowers that are very common. Never pick a wild flower unless there are at least eight other healthy specimens around it that you leave unpicked.)

• Think about the final effect you're after. For a chain that's dense in flowers (ideal for a crown), split the stalk close to the bloom. For a more spaced-out look, split the stalk closer to the root.

HOW TO MAKE A MELTING MOMENT

Melting Moments are delicious biscuits that seem to melt in the mouth. What makes these biscuits taste so good is that the recipe includes custard powder. You can eat them one at a time, but they are seriously delicious sandwiched together with butter icing in the middle. Yummy!

You Will Need:

- 175 g soft butter • 100 g icing sugar
- 175 g plain flour • 100 g custard powder
- ½ teaspoon of baking powder
- a pinch of salt • a bowl • a sieve
- a greased baking tray • a fork

WHAT TO DO

1. Turn the oven on to 180°C / 350°F / Gas Mark 4 (ask an adult to supervise whenever you use an oven).

2. In a bowl, mix together the butter and icing sugar until the mixture is nice and smooth.

3. Use a sieve to sift the flour, baking powder and custard powder into the bowl. Add the pinch of salt, too.

4. Carefully fold the dry ingredients into the butter mixture.

5. Take one teaspoon of mixture at a time and roll into a ball.

6. Place on a greased baking tray and press down the top of each ball with the prongs of a fork to flatten it a little.

7. Bake in the oven for 15 to 18 minutes – until the biscuits are lightly golden. Use oven gloves when you take them out of the oven.

Top Tip. If you want to sandwich two biscuits together, just mix together equal amounts of soft butter and icing sugar in a bowl. Spread the bottom of one biscuit with a teaspoon of the butter icing mixture, then press another biscuit on top.

HOW TO HAVE
PERFECT POSTURE

Check your posture in a mirror and follow these dos and don'ts.

- **DO** hold your neck straight from your hairline to your shoulders.

  - **DON'T** let your head jut forward and your neck curve. You should be able to balance a book on your head.

- **DO** relax your shoulders and keep your shoulder blades flat.

  - **DON'T** let your chest cave inwards. Pull your shoulders out and back, but don't let them rise towards your ears.

- **DO** keep your spine straight with just a small curve in the small of your back, not a deep hollow.

  - **DO** tuck in your bottom and pull in your stomach.

    - **DON'T** let your feet splay outwards or inwards.

HOW TO SPOT A MOVIE CLICHÉ

Next time you and your friends sit down to enjoy a movie-night with popcorn, why not rent a high school movie. See how many of these clichés you can spot.

- No one ever hiccups, sneezes, burps or coughs.

- There is always a group of pretty girls who are mean and selfish.

- No one has lots of spots.

- Football players ALWAYS go out with cheerleaders.

- Girls are allowed to wear loads of make-up to school, but it is special make-up that never rubs off or smudges. It is only the mean girl whose mascara runs when she cries.

- When everyone in the school starts to sing, there is always music playing that everyone dances to, and everyone always knows exactly what steps to do.

- Whenever children are left alone at home something goes wrong – things get broken, spilt, burnt or lost.

- Kids always have telephones in their bedrooms.

- When there is trouble, the heroine will tell a younger kid to hide and stay hidden until it is safe to come out. The little kid will never obey and will sneak out and be captured by the baddies.

• If there is a fight or a chase, kids can usually escape from adults by crawling between their legs.

• Boys and girls who have been friends for years will suddenly realise how gorgeous the other person is and fall head over heels in love.

• There is always a high school prom – at which mean girls get punished and heroines have a great time.

HOW TO PUT TOGETHER A SCHOOL-BAG BEAUTY KIT

Chances are you're not allowed to wear make-up at school, but there's nothing wrong with looking good while you're there. You certainly won't want to drag around a tonne of make-up with you, but there are a few things worth taking with you.

IN THE BAG

Grab yourself a pretty little bag to store your stash in – nothing too big – something the size of a pencil case will do perfectly. Now you are ready to collect the following items:

• A mini mirror – great for checking how you're looking and carrying out close-up beauty repairs, and also perfect for seeing what's going on behind you in class.

• A pack of tissues for blotting shiny skin and, um, wiping a runny nose.

• A lipsalve is great for keeping lips soft and smooth. Choose the cream type that comes in a little tube. You can also rub a tiny dot into your nails and cuticles to keep them strong.

• Medicated spot cover – essential if your skin's prone to sudden break-outs.

• A mini make-up brush– use it to apply spot cover – using your fingers will just spread infection.

• Pop in a pot of petroleum jelly or a tube of clear mascara – great for adding subtle definition to eyelashes and brows without a teacher noticing you're wearing make-up.

• A mini hairbrush will keep you neat and tidy. Wind a couple of hair elastics round the handle of your brush in case you want to swish your hair back into a ponytail later on.

• Carry a couple of pretty hair clips so that you can add pizzazz in an instant.

HOW TO MAKE A DISCO MIRROR BALL

A mirror ball is a great way to give any party some extra sparkle. Just follow these easy steps to make your own.

You Will Need:

• a round balloon • some newspapers • petroleum jelly
• wallpaper paste • a thick paintbrush • silver mirror card
(you can get this from a craft shop) • scissors • PVA glue
• a needle and some thick thread • black paint • sticky putty

Make A Papier-Mâché Ball. Blow up a round balloon to make a nice ball shape. Spread a thin layer of petroleum jelly all over the surface of the balloon (this will make it easier to remove later). Mix the wallpaper paste with water according to the instructions on the packet.

Tear up lots of strips of newspaper and stick them onto the balloon using plenty of wallpaper paste. Leave a big-enough space at the top of the balloon to fit your hand in.

Cover the balloon with at least four layers of newspaper, letting each layer dry before starting a new one.

Leave your papier-mâché ball to dry completely for a day or two. Then use a pin to pop the balloon and pull it out of the ball.

Paint The Ball Black. Use black acrylic or poster paint to cover all the newspaper on the ball. Leave to dry again.

Add Silver Squares. Cut the silver mirror card into lots of squares about 3 cm by 3 cm. Cover the ball in the squares using the PVA glue. Arrange the squares in nice neat rows, trimming any to fit awkward spaces. Your aim is to cover the entire ball – like a mosaic. When finished you should only be able to see a tiny bit of black paint peeking through.

Attach The Thread. Use a thick needle to pierce three holes about 2 cm below the opening of your ball. Space them at equal distances around the rim. (It's a good idea to hold a ball of sticky putty on the inside of the ball where you are making the hole and this will prevent you sticking the needle through your finger!)

Feed a length of strong thread through the needle and make sure you tie a big knot at the end. From the inside of the ball feed the needle through one of the holes. Use sticky tape to secure the knot to the inside of the ball. Repeat for each hole in your ball.

Party Time. Finally, use the three threads to hang up your mirror ball, give it a spin, and let the disco begin!

HOW TO PLAY THE FLOUR TOWER GAME

The Flour Tower Game guarantees serious fun for two or more players. It is probably best to play this one in the kitchen or the garden if you don't want to get told off for making a mess!

You Will Need:

- a shallow bowl full of flour • an unwrapped sweet
- a breadboard • a spoon

THE RULES

1. Fill the bowl with flour right to the rim – squishing the flour down hard with a spoon.

2. Put the breadboard over the top of the bowl and carefully flip them upside down – do this by holding one hand on top of the bowl and the other on the bottom of the board. The bowl should end up upside down on top of the board.

3. Oh-so-carefully lift the bowl, so that you're left with a bowl-shaped dome of flour on top of the breadboard.

4. Place the sweet on top of the flour dome.

5. Each player must take a turn to scoop away some flour with the spoon, without disturbing the sweet. This is easy to start with, but it soon gets more and more difficult as the flour is cut away, leaving a skinny tower with the sweet on top.

6. The player who makes the flour tower collapse and the sweet fall is the loser. Her punishment is to pick the sweet from the middle of the flour ... with her teeth – no hands allowed!

HOW TO MAKE A GARDEN ON A TRAY

You can have a whole garden on your bedroom windowsill if you create it on a tray. The basic method is described here, but remember that your garden's individual look totally depends on what you find to put in it.

GETTING STARTED

A gardener's seedling tray will make an ideal base for your garden, but any container that's around 50 cm by 25 cm and at least 5 cm deep will be fabulous.

Prepare the tray by lining the bottom of it with a sheet of plastic (using an old plastic bag works well). Cover the plastic with a fine layer of gravel (to help with drainage) and on top of that spread a thick layer of compost or soil from the garden.

CREATING THE LANDSCAPE

Plants. Small houseplants, mini cacti or flowers will be great as the main plants in your garden. Simply make a hole in the soil and pop them into place.

Pond. A small mirror or circle of aluminium foil makes a great pond. Cut tiny fish out of orange paper to 'swim' in it.

Rocks. Use pretty pebbles or stones to create mountains or boulders.

Grass. Moss from your garden makes great grass (don't pick it in the wild), or if you can't find any cut shapes out of green felt.

Pathway. Carefully use some gravel (the sort you can buy from a petshop to go in a fishbowl) or bark chippings to create a path in your garden. Make it as windy as you like.

THE FINISHING TOUCHES

It's the small details that will bring your mini garden to life.

- Add mini figures of people or animals to enjoy your garden.

- Various dolls' house items work well – a seat could be a garden bench, ornaments could be garden statues and a carpet could be a picnic rug.

- Make a washing line with two lolly sticks and some string – hang some dolls' clothes from it.

- Make a garden shed with a small box painted brown.

- Create a snowy effect by sprinkling your garden with salt. Why not add a snowman made from white modelling clay?

- Perhaps add some train track at the bottom of the garden with a train running along it.

HOW TO BREAK BAD BEAUTY HABITS

It's often the simplest things that give your looks a boost –
and the simplest things that can ruin them, too. Here's the
low-down on the bad beauty habits it is time to break.

Constantly Touching Your Face. All you're doing is rubbing
grime from your fingertips straight onto your skin –
encouraging spots and blemishes.

Twiddling Your Hair. If you absent-mindedly play with your
hair all the time, you're on a fast track to split ends.

Licking Your Lips. The truth is, licking your lips actually makes
them drier than ever and more prone to chapping. Keep a
delicious lipsalve handy and reach for it when your lips feel dry.

Rubbing Your Eyes. The skin around your eyes is very thin
and delicate – constantly rubbing it can leave it red and sore.

Picking Spots. Yuk! When you pick at a spot, you risk scarring
and spreading infection. Dab on some clay-based face pack or
a spot treatment overnight to dry it out.

Using Rubber Bands In Your Hair. Uncovered elastic bands tear
and split your hair. Use a proper fabric-coated band instead.
Rub a dot of conditioner onto the band beforehand to protect
your hair while you wear it.

Nibbling Your Nails. It's a hard habit to break, but worth it if
you want nice-looking hands. Try leaving one nail for biting

and painting the rest with a yucky-tasting no-bite liquid. As you gradually break the biting habit, paint the nail you left for biting, too.

Borrowing Make-Up. You might be desperate to share your friend's eyeliner pencil, but do you want to share her eye infection, too?

Sleeping With The Heating On High. If you don't want skin like a crocodile, try sleeping in a cooler room. Turn the heating down before bed – central heating makes the air so dry it'll sponge up moisture from your skin. If your parents insist on a boiling hot house, keep a well-watered pot plant in your room to keep the air moist.

Using Heated Hair-Styling Appliances Every Day. Straighteners, tongs and curlers are fine every now and again, but used every day they'll wreak havoc on your poor old locks. Only use them on dry hair, and protect it with a blow-dry spray before use. Let your hair dry naturally whenever you can to keep hair shiny and healthy.

HOW TO PLAY CAT'S CRADLE

Grab a friend and try out this string game. See how quickly you can get at performing the following sequence.

HOW TO PLAY

1. Tie a piece of string 160 cm long into a loop.

2. Slip both your hands, except your thumbs, inside the loop. Wrap the string around each hand again. With your middle finger hook the string which lies across the opposite palm from underneath and pull. Repeat with the other hand to make a 'Cat's Cradle'.

3. Using both her thumbs and index fingers, your friend should pinch the Cat's Cradle from above at the two points where the strings criss-cross.

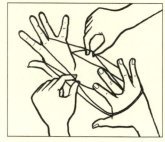

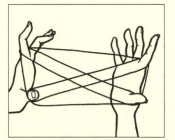

4. Your partner pulls the crosses out and around the outside strings. Then she scoops them up through the centre. Let the Cradle go so that she can pull it tight on her fingers. This is the 'Soldier's Bed'.

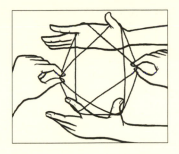

5. In exactly the same way, you must pinch the two points on the Soldier's Bed where the long strings cross.

6. Scoop them around and up through the centre.
As you draw the strings apart they will form four parallel lines.
This pattern is called 'Candles'.

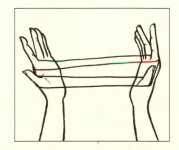

7. With the little finger of her right hand, your partner now hooks the string on the inside left, and with the little finger of her left hand, she hooks the string on the inside right. She pulls them out to make a square.

8. Your partner then scoops up the outside strings with both thumbs and index fingers making a 'Reverse Cradle'.

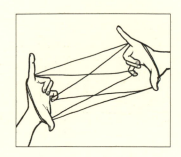

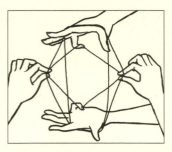

9. In the same way your friend made the Soldier's Bed, you must bring the crosses out and around the outside strings from underneath.

10. This time, go down into the centre, before pulling taut.

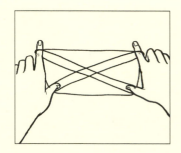

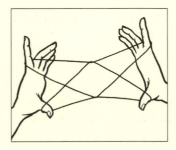

11. Your partner then repeats the actions you used to make Candles, but she magically creates a pattern of four triangles instead, called 'Cat's Eyes'.

12. Now put your thumbs and index fingers down into each of the triangles, scoop up through the centre and pull out to make a 'Fish In A Dish'.

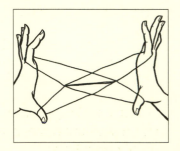

HOW TO MAKE PERFECT POPCORN

Question: How do you turn a boring night in front of the telly into a fun movie night?

Answer: Invite your friends over, switch on your favourite DVD and tuck into a huge bowl of homemade popcorn. Yummy!

Home-made popcorn takes minutes to make, tastes delicious and costs much less than the ready-made or microwave stuff you can buy from the supermarket. You'll find popcorn kernels by the dried beans and lentils in a supermarket or a healthfood shop.

All you need is a saucepan and an adult standing by (because things get hot).

WHAT TO DO

1. Find the biggest saucepan in the house – it must have a lid. Put it on the hob and pour in a tablespoon of oil (any sort of vegetable oil is fine).

2. Chuck in two handfuls of dry popcorn kernels.

3. Give the pan a good shake to spread the oil around.

4. Put the lid on and switch on the heat to medium.

5. Popcorn-making requires patience. Don't be tempted to sneak a peek under the lid or you may get hit on the nose by a flying corn missile!

6. Soon you'll hear the kernels popping and hitting the sides and lid of the saucepan. It gets very noisy!

7. When the noise dies down to only a couple of pops a second, turn off the heat.

8. When the popping has stopped completely, take off the lid and tip your delicious popcorn into a bowl.

GET SPRINKLING

Now it is time to add flavour to your basic popcorn. Choose one or more of these delicious toppings ...

- For classic corn, add a little salt.

- Sugar – any type will do, though brown sugar is especially nice.

- A spoon of golden syrup, runny honey or maple syrup. Add a handful of chopped nuts, too.
  (**Warning.** Don't add nuts if you are allergic to them.)

- A knob of butter. Stir well.

- Chilli powder or cayenne pepper – it's hot, hot, hot!

- Cocoa powder.

- Finely grated Parmesan cheese.

HOW TO WIN WHEN YOU PULL A CRACKER

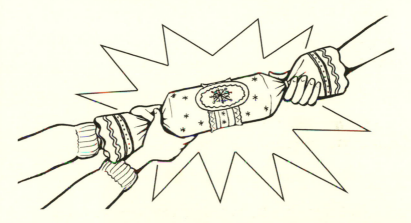

Scientists have spent hours working out the best way to win a cracker pull – which is a good job because crackers these days often contain great gifts that are worth winning.

The good news is it doesn't matter how big or small you are compared to your opponent – it's all in the technique. Experts say these tips will maximise your chances of securing the prize.

- Fix your opponent with a cool stare – this will unsettle them.

- Hold the cracker with a firm, two-handed grip to produce even pressure and prevent the cracker being torn.

- Tilt your end of the cracker downwards during the pull.

- Don't twist or use too much sudden force – aim for a steady and controlled pull instead.

HOW TO MAKE A SILHOUETTE PORTRAIT

People have made silhouette portraits of their friends and family for years – and they look really effective. Expert artists can cut out an image freehand, but this simple technique works brilliantly, too.

You Will Need:

- a sheet of white paper
- a sheet of black paper
- sticky putty • a lamp
- a pencil • scissors • glue

WHAT TO DO

1. Fix the sheet of white paper to a wall with some sticky putty.

2. Get your friend to sit in profile (sideways on) next to the wall. Place a bright lamp beside her (make sure your friend is between the lamp and the paper). Move the lamp back and forward until your friend's shadow profile appears on the white paper life-size and not blurred.

3. Use the pencil to trace around the shadow on the paper.

4. Take the sheet of white paper down from the wall and cut out the silhouette along the pencil line you have made.

5. Glue the silhouette on to a sheet of black paper – this will show it off to best effect.

HOW TO PLAY CLOCK WATCHERS

All you need for this game is an alarm clock and three or more players. Make sure you cover up any other clocks in the room and confiscate all watches and mobile phones!

Get everyone to stand in a circle. Set the alarm clock so that it will ring in about two minutes' time. The idea is for each player to sit down when they think the alarm is going to ring – they should shout out their name as they sit down. The last person to sit down before the alarm rings is the winner and anyone left standing after it has rung must pay a forfeit.

HOW TO SPOT YOUR FRIEND IS A WEREWOLF

If you have a niggling suspicion that on the night of a full moon your friend transforms herself into a wolf-like creature, see the checklist below. If she matches more than five of the criteria, it's time to panic because she's definitely a werewolf!

- She's hopeless at karaoke – she howls rather than sings.

- She's got red-tinged, curled fingernails.

- She gets restless whenever the moon becomes full.

- She never wears silver jewellery – silver is a metal feared by werewolves as they can only be killed by bullets made of it.

• There are reported sightings of a strange creature roaming your street that always coincide with evenings your friend is not around at your house.

• Your goldfish tries to jump out of its bowl when your friend is in your bedroom. Your pet puppy whimpers, particularly when your friend tries to eat the food from its bowl when no one is looking.

• It is embarrassing to go out for a meal with her because she picks up her food with her hands, rips it apart with her teeth, and snarls at the waiter.

• Tell your friend that the first sign of being a werewolf is hairy palms. Then tell her that the second sign of being a werewolf is looking for hair on your palms. Watch to see if she turns over her hands to check them.

HOW TO MAKE FANCY COCKTAILS

Invite a few friends round to enjoy some alcohol-free cocktails – known as 'mocktails'. Find out how to create some delicious drinks and decorate the glasses.

THE RECIPES

Seabreeze. Take a tall glass and add equal amounts of grapefruit juice and cranberry juice. Stir well and add plenty of crushed ice.

Green Monster. Squeeze the juice of a whole lime into a small glass. Top with lemonade and crushed ice. Add a slice of lime.

Cola Float. Pour some fizzy cola into a tall glass. Drop in two scoops of vanilla ice cream and stir.

St Clements. Pour equal amounts of orange juice and bitter lemon over crushed ice. Serve in a tall glass.

Cinderella. Mix together equal amounts of pineapple juice, apple juice and lemon juice. Pour into a tall glass and top up with fizzy lemonade.

THE DECORATION

Cocktails shouldn't just taste delicious, they should look good, too. Here are some ways to add some pizzazz to your drinks.

- Make coloured ice cubes by adding food colouring to water before freezing.

- Sugar-frost your glass before pouring in the drinks. Dip the rim in a little water, then in a saucer of caster sugar.

- Slices of fruit always look great. Make a small slit in a slice and balance on the rim of the glass.

- Pop in a pretty straw – the twirlier the better.

- Don't forget all the best mocktails are decorated with a paper umbrella.

HOW TO COLOUR CARNATIONS

Give someone a bunch of flowers in their favourite colour – even if it's blue, green or black!

You Will Need:

- six white carnations • 300 ml of water
- 20 drops of food colouring in the colour you want your flowers to be • a clear jar

WHAT TO DO

1. Pour the water into the jar and add the food colouring.

2. Cut about 5 cm off the base of the stems of your carnations, then stand them in the water.

3. Check every now and then, watching the flowers gradually change colour over the next 24 hours. Even though they haven't got roots, the stems of the flowers will suck up the coloured water and transport it to the flowers and leaves.

4. If your carnations don't start to show colour in the petals within six hours, add some more food colouring to the water.

Top Tip. Red and blue food colouring work the best.

HOW TO BE A SYNCHRONIZED SWIMMER

If you're strong, flexible and good at holding your breath underwater, synchronized swimming may be the perfect sport for you. It's all about performing routines in the water in complete harmony with the other swimmers in your squad.

IMPRESS THE JUDGES

Here are the ten steps to follow to become a top synchronized swimmer – guaranteed to impress the judges every time.

1. Decide whether you're going to work as a pair or in a team. A maximum of eight girls can be in a team. Starting in a pair, known as a duet, is a good idea as it's easier to keep in time with one person than with a whole group.

2. Dress right. Make sure your team wears matching swimming cossies. Sweep your hair back into neat buns with matching scrunchies.

3. Pop on a nose clip – essential to stop the water rushing up your nose when making upside-down underwater moves!

4. Choose your music carefully – anything with a good beat is great, especially songs from musicals.

Warning. It is essential that you keep musical equipment well away from the poolside.

5. Make a good impression on the judges before you even get in the pool by performing some fancy 'deckwork'. These are

the movements done on the side of the pool before you enter the water. But be quick – you're only allowed 10 seconds of deckwork before you get in the pool.

6. Never touch the bottom of the pool with your hands or feet during the routine – the judges will penalise you.

7. Practise keeping your eyes open under water – you need to be able to check what your teammates are doing.

8. Practise holding your breath under water. The top synchronized swimmers can stay under for up to a minute while performing complicated moves.

9. Practise the basic moves until they're second nature. Check out the mini guide on page 112.

10. Smile! Even if you're really exhausted, it's essential to smile and convince the audience that the display is easy-peasy.

THE ESSENTIAL MOVES

Here's a guide to the main moves in this sport.

Boost. A speedy head-first rise out of the water where you aim to raise as much of your body as possible above the surface.

Cadence Action. A sequence of movements performed one-by-one by all team members, usually in rapid succession.

Twirl. A rapid twist of 180 degrees.

Ballet Leg. Each swimmer lies flat on the surface with one leg flat on the water and the other stretched straight up in the air.

Egg-beater. A leg kick which supports your whole body, leaving your arms free.

Vertical Position. This is when you position yourself upside down in the water, without touching the bottom. Your legs point straight up and out of the water – point those toes!

HOW TO MAKE
A DANCING-QUEEN CARD

Use the template opposite to make a gorgeous greetings card.

You Will Need:

- tracing paper (greaseproof paper will do)
- a pencil • some thin card • scissors • a needle
- four butterfly paper-fasteners • felt-tip pens

WHAT TO DO

1. Trace the queen's head and body, legs and arms on page 113.

2. Place the tracing paper over the top of the card (use some tape to keep the tracing paper in place). Draw over the pencil lines again, pressing firmly so it leaves an indented mark on the card (draw the big dots where the holes will go, too).

3. Remove the tracing paper and go over the marks on the card with the pencil, then cut out the card shapes.

4. Pierce the big holes with the end of the scissors – ask an adult for help here to prevent pierced fingers!

5. Attach each of the legs and arms to the body of the queen with a butterfly paper-fastener.

6. Colour in the queen, drawing in her features. Write a greeting on the back of the card. Pop it in an envelope and post it to your friend.

HOW TO INTERPRET YOUR DREAMS

Experts say your dreams will give you clues about who you are and reveal your deepest emotions. Here are some of the most common dreams and what some people believe your inner mind is trying to tell you when you dream them.

You're At School With No Clothes On. This means you feel exposed. Perhaps you've started at a new school or a new class and feel unprepared? Don't worry, you'll make friends and learn the ropes soon.

You're Flying. This lovely dream means you're feeling creative, confident and strong.

Your Teeth Fall Out. This common dream means you've been feeling very self-conscious about your appearance – perhaps you've recently made some new friends and wonder what they think about you. Relax ... next time you see them, just smile and have a good time.

You're In A Beautiful Garden. You're feeling calm, happy and stable.

You're Falling. This probably means you're feeling worried and insecure about something, such as finishing a project in time. Make sure you haven't taken on too much so you don't feel overwhelmed.

You See A Rainbow. This reveals your hope for success in the future – a rainbow forms a bridge between what's happening today and what will happen tomorrow.

You've Lost Something Important. Convinced you have lost your house key or purse? This means you're worried about losing your position as best at something. Or maybe you've fallen out with a friend and need to make up.

You're Giving Money Away. This means you're a loving person.

You Dream About Your Teacher. You may be seeking advice, support or guidance about something that's worrying you.

HOW TO MAKE POT POURRI

Put together some pot pourri – a mixture of dried flowers, herbs, spices and citrus fruits. It not only looks pretty but it will make your bedroom smell nice, too. Here's what you can use:

FLOWERS

Any sweet-smelling flowers will do, though roses are particularly lovely. Get permission before you pick any flowers from the garden or ask at the local florist for any discarded flowers and buds they don't need. Place the flower heads, buds or petals in a warm, airy spot to dry out for a few days.

HERBS

Herbs with woody stems are the best to use as they're highly perfumed and dry well – try lavender or rosemary. Hang bunches to dry in an airy spot for around a week. Healthfood shops are a good source of ready-dried lavender, or you may be lucky enough to have some growing in your garden.

SPICES

Ready-dried spices will really enhance the smell of your pot pourri and look great, too. The best ones to try are cinnamon sticks, cloves and star anise. Ask if there are any out-of-date spices in the kitchen cupboard – they might not be good to eat but they're still fine to use for pot pourri.

FRUIT

Dried fruit slices look pretty and have a wonderful scent. You can buy them ready-made or make them by slicing a citrus fruit finely and drying the slices out in an oven at a low

temperature for a couple of hours. A mixture of lemons, limes and oranges look really great.

Mix all your pot pourri ingredients together.

Take your time arranging them in a pretty bowl. Any bowl will do, although wooden or glass bowls really emphasise the natural look of pot pourri. Then place on a low table and enjoy!

ADDED EXTRAS

The wonderful thing about homemade pot pourri is you can keep adding to the mixture to change the way it looks and smells – for instance, you could include pretty pine cones, small seashells, miniature Christmas decorations or pieces of bark.

Why not add a few drops of perfume oil after a while, when the natural scent of your pot pourri starts to fade?

HOW TO MAKE YOUR OWN ICE LOLLIES

Home-made lollies are easy to make, especially if you get your hands on a plastic lolly mould. All you need to do is fill the mould up, pop it in the freezer and wait. If you haven't got a special lolly mould, use clean mini yogurt pots. Here are some great recipes.

BANANA & HONEY

Mash up some banana. Mix it with milk and a delicious squirt of runny honey.

LOVELY LEMONADE

Add a squeeze of fresh lemon to some ordinary lemonade.

SMOOTHIE MOVE

Just pour in some of your favourite smoothie drink.

FRESH & FRUITY

Simply mix equal quantities of fruit yogurt and fruit juice.

CHOCOLATE HEAVEN

Make up some hot chocolate from cocoa powder and milk. Allow to cool before pouring into the moulds.

Top Tips. Avoid pineapple – anything with pineapple in it won't freeze. Before your lolly mix is completely frozen, remove it from the freezer. Add a clean lolly stick to the middle of the mixture – so you can hold your lolly later when it's frozen.

HOW TO SLICE A BANANA WITHOUT PEELING IT

Give your friend a major surprise when she peels a banana and finds that it is already miraculously cut into four pieces. She won't believe her eyes.

1. Simply thread a long needle with cotton. Push the needle under the skin of the banana and wiggle it along the inside edge of the skin, as shown, until it comes out.

2. Push the needle back through the same hole and carry on wiggling. Repeat until you've slipped the thread right round the whole banana, and brought the needle out through the original hole.

3. Hold both ends of the thread together and pull out – this will cut the banana inside the skin. Do this three times down the length of the banana. Pop the banana in your lunchbox and offer it to your friend at break time.

HOW TO MAKE A SLEDGE GO FASTER

Here are some essential tips for safe and speedy sledging.

While you need boots with a good grip to stop you slipping over in icy weather, you want the opposite when it comes to your sledge. The smoother the base of your sledge, the better. The best way to reduce friction between your sledge and the snow is to rub the underside with candle wax, vegetable oil or some furniture polish.

You'll pick up the fastest speeds on areas of ground where the ice is really packed down – going down the same path several times will do the trick, or follow in the tracks of people who started sledging before you.

SAFETY TIPS

- Get permission first ... and make sure an adult knows where you're sledging.

- Only sledge in a safe area – avoid roads, driveways and clifftops!

- Don't sledge in the dark.

- Don't sledge straight into a large mound of snow unless you know the area well – it might hide a tree stump or barbed wire.

- Learn how to stop your sledge or make a sharp turn by dragging your feet.

Top Tip. If your sledge won't stop or you're out of control, roll off it onto the ground. Don't worry about your sledge – you can get it once it stops sliding.

HOW TO MAKE A SNOW SHAKER

Snow shakers are easy to make and make gorgeous gifts – though you'll probably want to keep them for yourself when you've made them. The brilliant thing about snow shakers is that you can put anything in them.

What You Need:

- a jam jar with a water-tight screw-top lid
(soak the jar in warm soapy water to peel off the label)
- a bottle of glycerine (a syrupy liquid found in chemists and the cookery section of supermarkets)
- water • a spoon • a jug • some glitter
- a lump of sticky putty • small plastic toys or decorations (what goes inside the snow shaker is up to you – you can use anything so long as it will to be okay submerged in water)

WHAT TO DO

Here's how to make your own snow shaker.

1. Stick a lump of sticky putty to the inside of the jam jar's lid. Mould the sticky putty into a hill shape – making sure you leave a gap around the edges so you'll be able to screw it back onto the jar later on.

2. Now it's time to create your snow shaker scene. Stick a plastic toy into the top of the sticky putty. Make sure it will stay put even when held upside down or shaken.

3. Add equal parts of water and glycerine to a jug. Add a tablespoon of glitter to your mixture. This will be the snow in your shaker. The glycerine will ensure the glitter 'snow' moves slowly in the water.

4. Pour your 'snow' mixture into the jam jar.

5. Holding your jam jar over a sink in case of spills, twist on the lid – being careful not to dislodge the figure from the sticky putty.

6. Turn the jar upside down, shake and watch the snow swirl around your scene.

Top Tip. If you're making snow shakers as gifts, tailor them to the occasion – add hearts for Valentine's Day, mini decorations for Christmas and bunnies for Easter.

HOW TO BLOW AN EGG

If you want to decorate eggs and display them permanently as ornaments, you need to blow out the contents first otherwise they'll start to smell. Here's how to do it.

1. Wash and dry the egg gently.

2. Very carefully puncture a tiny hole at the pointed end of the egg using a needle.

3. Now make a bigger hole at the round end of the egg. Push the needle right in to make sure you puncture the yolk.

4. Place the egg over a bowl and put your lips to the small hole, blowing until all the contents come out. (Take care not to suck out any of the contents and don't waste them – use them to make an omelette or scrambled eggs.)

5. Rinse the shell with cold water and allow it to dry thoroughly before painting it. You can use paints, felt-tip pens, wax crayons or food colouring to decorate your egg.

6. Paint on a coat of clear varnish to protect your decorations, harden the egg and ensure it stays beautiful forever.

HOW TO PLAY FIVESTONES

Fivestones is an ancient game, played by girls just like you for many centuries. You can play Fivestones on your own or compete with a friend. All you need is five plastic or metal jacks (you can buy these in toyshops) or you could use five stones each about the size of a penny.

WHAT TO DO

There are lots of different ways of playing Fivestones – this is a method that combines different skills.

To start, throw all five stones into the air with one hand and catch as many as you can on the back of the same hand.

Next, throw up all the stones that are on the back of your hand and try to catch them again in the palm of the same hand. If you end up with no stones in your hand and all of them on the ground, your turn is over.

If you managed to catch at least one stone you can continue playing. Keep one of the stones in your hand and scatter all the others on the ground.

Throw up the stone in your hand and quickly pick up one of the stones from the ground. Catch the stone in the air before it falls to the ground. Do this for each of the stones on the ground.

Repeat this, but this time pick up two stones before catching the tossed stone. On the second throw, pick up the two remaining stones.

Repeat, picking up three stones and one stone. Then finally pick up all four stones before catching the tossed stone.

The aim is to get through all the moves without dropping any stones.

When you are good enough to do this, try adding in a clap or a knee slap before picking up stones.

HOW TO AMAZE YOURSELF

Here are two 'tricks' to try out when you are alone that will amaze you. Once you know how to do them, perform them in front of your friends. They will all be convinced that you have magical powers.

LEVITATE YOUR ARM

Stand with both arms straight down by your sides. Move so you are standing beside a wall, with your right arm against it. Push the back of your right hand against the wall. Push hard while you count to 30. Now quickly step away from the wall and turn so that your back is to the wall. Watch as your arm mysteriously floats upwards.

LONG ARM, SHORT ARM

Now stretch your right arm out to the side of your body as far as you can reach. Move so that the tips of the fingers on your right hand are just touching the wall. Now bend your right arm, so the fingers touch your shoulder. With your other hand rub your elbow. Then straighten your right arm again. You will find that it has mysteriously 'shrunk' and you fingertips won't touch the wall. Weird!

IT'S NOT MAGIC

The thing is there is no magic involved in these two tricks. The movements of your bones, joints and muscles are what make them work.

ALSO AVAILABLE

The Girls' Book: How To
Be The Best At Everything
ISBN: 978-1-905158-79-9

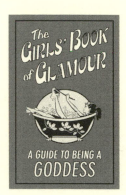

The Girls' Book Of Glamour:
A Guide To Being A
Goddess
ISBN: 978-1-906082-13-0

The Boys' Book: How To
Be The Best At Everything
ISBN: 978-1-905158-64-5

The Boys' Book 2:
How To Be The Best At
Everything Again
ISBN: 978-1-906082-33-8

The Boys' Book Of Survival:
How To Survive
Anything, Anywhere
ISBN: 978-1-906082-12-3

13738016R00076

Printed in Great Britain
by Amazon.co.uk, Ltd.,
Marston Gate.